Tee-ology

Tee-ology

·18·
Inspirational Lessons
for Golfers

JOHN FREEMAN

OLIVER
NELSON

THOMAS NELSON PUBLISHERS
Nashville • Atlanta • London • Vancouver

Published in Nashville, Tennessee, by Thomas Nelson, Inc., Publishers, and distributed in Canada by Word Communications, Ltd., Richmond, British Columbia, and in the United Kingdom by Word (UK), Ltd., Milton Keynes, England.

Library of Congress Cataloging-in-Publication Data

Freeman, John, 1946 Nov. 26–
    Tee-ology : 18 inspirational lessons for golfers / John Freeman.
      p. cm.
    ISBN 0-7852-7677-7 (hc)
    1. Golfers—Religious life.   2. Christian life.   3. Golf—
Religious aspects—Christianity.   I. Title.
BV4596.G64F74   1996
248.8′8—dc20   95–40966
                                          CIP

Printed in the United States of America

1 2 3 4 5 6 7 — 03 02 01 99 98 97 96

To

Levy:
golf partner,
ministry mentor,
father in the faith

Contents

Acknowledgments

These essays, written for the purpose of catharsis after enduring publishers' rejections of a much larger, more "serious" manuscript, were never intended to see the light of day. That they eventually did is due to the encouragement of a number of friends and colleagues to whom I owe thanks.

The idea to publish germinated at Lake Junaluska, North Carolina, where it was nurtured by a number of people. Special thanks go to Jim Warren, director of the Intentional Growth Center at the Lake, and his professional and volunteer staff, who did all the necessary tasks to develop the project. Bill Rogers supported the work with a generous financial gift. Ralph Bugg helped with his editorial expertise. My wife, Julie, and my daughter, Caroline, got the manuscript in publication shape. Scott Waxman helped it find an audience.

As far as content is concerned, I drew on many sources, the chief of which I salute here: my late father, who instilled the love of the game in me; the golfing saints of Trinity United Methodist Church in North

Myrtle Beach, South Carolina, who provided me lots of opportunities to see the connections between golf and faith; my Candler School of Theology colleague, Don Saliers, whose conversation to, from, and on the golf course has always delighted and enriched me; and Julie and Caroline, who, besides doing the heavy lifting on the computer, have indulged me in my passion for golf and upbuilt me by their exemplary faith.

I conclude by thanking the Reverend Levy Rogers, to whom the book is dedicated. Without his encouragement, imagination, and persistence this project would not have come to pass. Thanks, too, to his wife, Ruth, whose love has meant much to my family and me over the years.

Tee-ology

1

The Shot That Brings Us Back

". . . Since all have sinned and
fall short of the glory of God;
they are now justified by
his grace as a gift, through
the redemption that is
in Christ Jesus."
Romans 3:23–24

The Shot That
Brings Us Back

W E'VE ALL appeared in this scene. The day is
glorious, the course lush, and the camaraderie delightful.
We step onto the practice green and sink putt after putt.
As we limber up, we feel so good we can hardly wait
to get to the first tee. We rejoice and are glad, not only
because this is a day the Lord has made, but also because we feel a personal best round coming on.

Befitting the moment, we break out a new Titleist,
the kind of ball one reserves for just such an occasion.
With anticipation we set up to launch our first drive,
fully expecting to produce the monster fairway-splitter
pictured in our mind's eye. Instead, a topped roller dies
just beyond the ladies' tee box.

Not what we had in mind, but that's okay. It's a
forgiving hole, wide open and not too long, so we can

still salvage par. A bladed two-iron, a fat wedge, and a three-putt later, however, and our hopes crash and burn. It gets worse, so bad, in fact, that by the time we finish the front nine, our dream has turned into a nightmare, one pitiful par drowning in a sea of double and triple bogeys.

If it weren't for a sense of social obligation to our partners, we'd end our misery by quitting at the turn, but we trudge on, determined to recoup a measure of respectability on the back nine. Unfortunately, the disaster continues to the point that we consider giving up the game altogether, or at least we plan to take a long layoff, effective immediately.

As we start down the home stretch, a small miracle occurs. Up to now we've made all kinds of adjustments—stronger grip, more inside swing path, shorter backswing, wider stance—trying desperately to get back in the groove, when suddenly we pinpoint the problem. We know we've done so when we hit our best drive of the day on number sixteen, which we proceed to par. On seventeen we leave a birdie putt an inch shy of dead center, and on eighteen we close out with a solid par.

Talk about a mood swing! After spending most of the day in golfer's purgatory, we finish the round feeling like Lazarus raised from the grave. The awful memory of our struggles is displaced by the joy of finally getting things right. Forget about a layoff; we're ready to go to eighteen more holes right then.

The term "redemption" aptly fits such an experience. Even though we rally too late to redeem this round, our closing surge has rescued our attitude toward ourselves and the game, indeed toward life in general. The course may have won the battle today, but we do manage to retire with our dignity intact, eager to fight another day. There's a personal best score yet to be shot, and thanks to our strong finish, it still seems imminent. This is how redemption works—it turns despair into its opposite, hope.

As Paul teaches in Romans, redemption works the same way in the relationship between God and the world. That relationship, which was perfect at the time of Creation, was broken as soon as humans acted on their inclination to sin. Paul makes no bones about this being the starting point for reflection on the bond between humankind and God: "Since all have sinned and fall short of the glory of God . . ."

If sin had the final word, we would know nothing but despair, for our sin would perpetually distance us from God. Fortunately, Paul asserts, God has acted in Jesus Christ to justify us in spite of our sin, replacing our unrighteousness with his perfect righteousness, thereby making us acceptable in God's sight.

Paul calls this divine action "redemption." The word

literally means "a loosing away," the state of being set free from oppressive circumstances. Experiencing redemption is like feeling shackles fall off. When we personally lay claim to the gift of salvation, the deliverance from sin God makes available to us in Jesus Christ, we are redeemed. This doesn't mean we'll never sin again, or that our sin will no longer grieve both God and ourselves; it does mean we no longer have to be controlled by sin. Just as an abortive round of golf can be salvaged by a few good shots, God can redeem our lives, no matter how messy, from the domination of sin. There may be times when we think this is impossible, when all seems hopelessly lost, but from God's perspective it is never so.

Too good to be true? Not for us golfers. We know the joy of having a rotten game turn around. The good shots keep us coming back; that the bad shots don't make us give up in disgust shows we have experienced the game's power to redeem. Since we golfers know that redemption is not too good to be true, do you think God might have a special witness for us to make to those who haven't learned this marvelous lesson from our beloved game?

2

Tempo

"The wind blows where it
chooses, and you hear the
sound of it, but you do not
know where it comes from
or where it goes. So it
is with everyone who is
born of the Spirit."

John 3:8

Tempo

GOLF IS a simple game—get the ball in the hole with a minimum of strokes. Consider how best to accomplish this, however, and we see a simple game transforming into a complex science. Witness the world of swing theories. Whether we're trying to build from scratch or retool, we have many available options from which to choose. For example, we can try "square to square," "swing the handle rather than the clubhead," "the golf motor," "the big muscle method," or "pull the rope."

Golf gurus churn out such methods continually because they know we golfers are endlessly questing for the perfect swing. Having experimented with a number of these theories in my time, I feel qualified to offer one generalization: Every theory affirms, explicitly or implicitly, that the golf swing consists of two dimensions, one mechanical, the other mystical.

The mechanical dimension, while more technical, is easier to comprehend. It has to do with the physical positions and movements the golfer must learn in order to produce an efficient swing. Grip, stance, alignment, posture, balance, ball position, swing initiating procedures, plane, release, and follow-through are aspects of this category. Because swing mechanics can be complex, it's possible that they may bog one down, even to the point of paralysis. However, once the golfer has internalized the basics, this problem usually minimizes itself. The trick is to figure out what's most critical for one's individual swing and groove it in without worrying excessively about the rest. Most golfers who have the inclination and opportunity to practice can develop familiar, if not always trustworthy, swing mechanics.

The mystical dimension is another story. I'm referring here to swing tempo—the rhythm with which one moves the club away from, into, and through the ball. All the theories, no matter how diverse, acknowledge that mechanics must be executed with proper tempo for the swing to succeed, but I know of no foolproof method for causing this to happen. If you run into a method offering a guarantee at this point, cross it off your list, because it's making a promise it can't keep. Tempo is not so much a teachable position or movement as it is an innate quality in each individual golfer. This is why I call it the mystical dimension. It can hardly be described, much less prescribed. We can only say that good tempo is the quality that integrates the swing, enabling all the moving parts to work together to produce proper clubhead speed and position at the point of impact. Tempo may be slow or fast, depending on the individual's temperament. Speed up Jack Nicklaus's tempo—he'd never have won all those tournaments. Slow down Arnold Palmer's tempo—he'd have fizzled too. A natural attribute that each golfer has to discover and harness for himself, tempo cannot be imposed from without but must emerge from within.

There's a similar mystical dimension to the Christian life. Jesus attempts to explain this to Nicodemus when he tells him he must be born again. As the ensuing conversation shows, Nicodemus is baffled by this notion. A ruler of the Pharisees, Nicodemus is a decent, upright, God-fearing man, but his understanding of what it means to be religious is mechanistic. For him religion consists of pleasing God by observing the law; thus, he is a master of good deeds, attending scrupulously to the letter of the law. He knows and practices its mechanics, its institutionalized rituals and activities.

When Jesus introduces the necessity of being born again, Nicodemus finds himself at sea, because Jesus is not commending outward acts of compliance with religious rules, but an inward attitude of submission to, and utter trust in, God. This inward attitude, which provides the impetus for the deeds of love and justice God requires, comes from the Holy Spirit, over which humans have no control; rather, this attitude is a gift the Spirit implants in the receptive believer's heart. To be born again is to receive this gift, allowing it to take control of one's life. How, when, and where this happens can't be nailed down, because the Spirit, like the wind, is a mystery. Accordingly, true religion is not first and foremost a human achievement; it is embracing a possibility that God offers, a possibility that stirs within us because of the mysterious work of the Spirit.

The mystical dimension of religion that Jesus so wanted Nicodemus to grasp, he commends to you and me too. Although being a Christian entails doing the right things, such obedience is impossible unless we open ourselves to the Spirit of God, which not only reveals but also empowers us to fulfill God's will.

This is the mystical dimension of faith. We can pray, study, give, and work the best in the world, but if those actions aren't impelled by the right tempo—the attitude that God plants in us by the Holy Spirit—they will build vanity, not faith. Only if we allow the Holy Spirit to set our tempo will our faith mechanics fall into place. If this sounds mysterious, that's because it is—just like tempo in golf.

3

No Sandbagging!

". . . Should we continue
in sin in order that grace
may abound? By no means!"
Romans 6:1–2

No Sandbagging!

IT STARTS innocently enough. Discovering an unplayable lie, we kick the ball toward the fairway to give ourselves a swing. Or on the sly we take an extra "mulligan." Or we refuse to count the additional stroke for a lost ball because the rough, in our opinion, is not cut sufficiently. Or we disregard the out-of-bounds marker on account of our philosophical objection to unnatural hazards.

Gradually, and probably imperceptibly, we grant ourselves a selective exemption from the rules of golf. I don't imply that we become blatant outlaws; we don't disregard the tee markers, use the "hand wedge" out of the bunker, or give ourselves ten-foot putts. But we do slip into the habit of subtly bending the rules. The one thing we improve in the process isn't our game, but the skill of rationalizing, going through the mental contortions necessary to justify our actions.

But this fudging happens so seldom, it may be argued. Sure, we all give ourselves a break now and then, but what's the harm, so long as we don't really hurt anybody or turn the game into chaos? It isn't a big deal unless the golfer is a professional, in which case the rules must be strictly observed. But for us amateurs, live and let live. After all, it's only a game.

It is, indeed, only a game, but, more than most games, doesn't the way we play golf accurately reflect the way we live off the course? I believe this is especially true concerning our penchant for rationalizing. Show me a golfer who has ready excuses for weaseling out of his bad shots, and I'll show you an accountant who may doctor the books, a contractor who may inflate material costs, or a parent who may default on promises made to her children.

In golf, such rationalizing leads to cheating; in life, it leads to sin. Sin is not just the bad things we do or the good things we fail to do. It is also the sly thought process, sometimes conscious but frequently unconscious, that leads to harmful behavior. Like an unchecked disease, such sinful rationalizing infects every aspect of our lives, even our religion. As with the rules of golf, we can twist the Christian faith to suit ourselves, in the process warping the divine truth upon which it is founded.

Consider, for example, the matter of grace, God's unmerited, inexhaustible love for the world that is perfectly communicated by Jesus Christ. God sent Jesus so that grace might supplant law as the power governing all relationships. As the perfect embodiment of God's grace, Jesus liberated people from the dead letter of the law, setting them free to live by the vibrant spirit of grace. This good news, which we call "the gospel," is the great gift Jesus brought into the world.

With the help of God, even one so committed to the old way of the law as Paul was able to embrace the new way of grace. After working through the upheaval of radical change in his own life resulting from his personal encounter with the gospel, he began to spread the message of grace to others. It probably didn't surprise him to encounter resistance from people who, like himself, were staunch advocates of the law. More of a problem, perhaps, were people who seized upon his message of grace and made it carte blanche for their own selfish desires instead of understanding grace as God intended: a liberation for the service of outpouring love. When they heard that grace had replaced law as the rule for living, their rationalizing ran wild. "Hot dog! Now I can do anything I want and not worry, because I'm covered by grace—in fact, according to this gospel that

Paul preaches, the more I sin, the more grace I get. What a deal!"

Paul pulls no punches when he replies with a thunderous, "By no means!" If we understand God's grace and truly receive it, Paul elaborates, we become different persons, no longer captive to sin. To accept the gift of grace is to resolve to die to sin, and we can't do that without first dying to the rationalizing process that precedes the transgressions themselves.

This is part of Paul's great theme that we are justified, or saved, not by our own efforts but by the grace of God, which we receive through faith in Jesus Christ. We focus here on his reminder that while grace is free, it is not cheap. It comes by virtue of Jesus' suffering and dying for our sake. Whoever would claim God's grace, therefore, may not play fast and loose with it, as we do when we rationalize.

So maybe there is more at stake than we realize when we ponder whether to nudge the ball away from the bush or to dismiss the whiff as a practice swing. More insidious than our reducing our score or inflating our handicap is the real sin of building up our rationalizing muscle, making it harder to subdue on the job, with our family and friends, in our religious life.

If we think grace winks at that—"By no means!" Only when we allow grace to defeat our tendency to rationalize can we know its true meaning and realize its full benefits. That's when the victory over sin begins. Is there a better place to practice this kind of straight shooting than on the golf course?

4

It's Not the Equipment

"Jesus Christ is the same
yesterday and today
and forever."
Hebrews 13:8

It's Not the
Equipment

To ALLOW square grooves or not to allow square grooves, that is the question. The grooves issue has commanded major attention in the golfing community for some time now. For those who may not know the background, the Karsten Manufacturing Company, maker of Ping golf clubs, produced a set of irons featuring square grooves on the clubface, which supposedly impart more backspin on the ball than clubs with standard grooves. More backspin means greater accuracy and control; therefore, officials of the Professional Golf Association, believing such clubs constitute an unfair advantage, sought to outlaw them on the pro tour. Ping has successfully fought this action in the courts, sparking plenty of conversation in clubhouses all over America.

That such a controversy erupted is no surprise. The

last quarter century has produced quantum leaps in equipment technology. The Ping brouhaha really is a sign of a growing concern that the game's nature is being threatened by the ever-increasing use of space-age materials and designs for both clubs and balls. I think about the changes I have seen since I took up the game. Initially, tubular steel shafts and wooden clubheads were the norm. In the interim I've seen fiberglass, aluminum, "lite" steel, graphite, titanium, and all sorts of composites come along, each promising to revolutionize the game. There are forged and investment-cast irons, as well as laminated, solid, metal, and graphite/composite "woods." Every year, it seems, I hit a new ball with a tougher cover and more dimples in a greater variety of configurations, all of which guarantee added length. Even putters have evolved. Where once the simple blade and mallet-head held sway, the field is now crowded with shapes, colors, lengths, angles, and materials, some of which would make former masters turn over in their graves. Can you picture Bobby Jones, for example, using the extralong putter popular on today's scene?

The many improvements are not an unmixed blessing. As the large collection of putters gathering dust in my closet testifies, the surfeit of equipment options can be confusing—and expensive. We rush out and buy the latest "breakthrough," only to discover that the miraculous result promised by advertisement or salesperson is illusory. So after three erratic rounds we retire the shiny new graphite driver and exhume the scarred, old, laminated two-wood we depended on for years. We swear never to divorce her again—at least not until another wonder club hits the market.

To put it another way, while the advances may noticeably benefit a few, they will likely have little effect on most of us. This is because, as one knowledgeable observer put it, "It doesn't matter how square the grooves are; if you can't put a decent swing on the ball to begin with, all the good stuff that club's supposed to do will never happen." The best equipment in the world, used improperly, won't elevate our game an inch.

In other words, if improvement is to occur, something must remain constant in the midst of all the flux. The more sound and consistent a golfer's swing, the greater chance he has to benefit from "advanced" equipment. But if he changes his grip or his stance or his tempo as often as he experiments with a new shaft, little good will result. In the midst of change, some things must remain constant, lest chaos rule.

Since the beginning God has been trying to lead humankind from the confusion and alienation it has inflicted on itself. God's love would, if universally embraced, deliver the world from this chaos. The Bible teaches that God offered this love through law, prophecy, wisdom, and ultimately through the person and work of Jesus Christ. In Christ the love of God abides, because Christ is a living reality, as the writer of Hebrews says, "yesterday and today and forever."

We will live through many changes, some threatening to crush us, others promising to exalt us. We may not think we can handle the death of a child, the end of a career, the loss of health; on the other hand, we may believe that the joy we have been searching for is finally about to be realized in our new love, our recently acquired wealth, even the new church home that feels so warm and inviting. In the swirl of changes, good and bad, we ask, what abides? For the Christian the answer is always the same: Jesus Christ, God's incarnate love, that comes to us as both sustenance and challenge in the midst of change. He is the constant who assures that no matter how despairing or exciting we find the changes that confront us, we can deal with them without fear of being swept away by chaos.

Life, like golf clubs, changes over time. Because we cling to that which abides, life's changes don't throw us. We greet them with courage, for we know that as long as we depend on the love of God in Jesus Christ, we master the changes; they don't master us.

5

Prepared for All Circumstances

". . . the kingdom of heaven
will be like this. Ten
bridesmaids took their
lamps and went to meet the
bridegroom. Five of them were
foolish, and five were wise. . . .
The wise took flasks of oil
with their lamps."

Matthew 25:1-2, 4

Prepared for All Circumstances

WHEN, SOME years ago, my bishop appointed me to serve Trinity United Methodist Church on South Carolina's Grand Strand resort coast, I felt like the luckiest minister in Christendom. To be assigned to a vibrant congregation filled with golfers and located in a golfing paradise—what more could a golfing preacher want?

Here my golf was transformed from a hobby into a ministry. Because many of my parishioners played the game, I found myself doing much of my pastoral visitation on the course. The arrangement seemed to please them, and I certainly loved it.

I had the opportunity then to play a lot of golf with women, who made up a significant percentage of my golfing flock. In doing so I was disabused of several stereotypes of the woman golfer. I discovered, for example, that she is not necessarily more interested in the social rather than physical part of the game. She is just as likely to take a hard swing as a man of comparable age and health. She is not ignorant of the rules. And she tends to be, if anything, more competitive than the male of the species, as I learned when my golfing sisters refused to concede the "gimme" putts men routinely give each other.

I would venture one general observation, however, which I am convinced is fact, not stereotype. When women play golf, they are prepared for any eventuality. In extreme cases their golf carts resemble the wagons of old-time peddlers. I know this firsthand because my female golfing companions often shared their provisions with me. At one time or another they provided me with all manner of food and drink; they kept me warm with afghans, mufflers, mittens, and stocking caps; they attended to my medical needs with everything from aspirin to bandages; they lent me ball retrievers to fish stray shots out of the water; they supplied me binoculars for scouting distant pin placements.

I make no explanation of this. I only observe that women, unlike men, are seldom unprepared for whatever contingencies arise on the course. Though merely curious at first, I soon came to appreciate this trait of the woman golfer, especially since I often benefited from her largesse.

When I reminisce about those experiences, I am reminded of Jesus' parable of the wise and foolish maidens. Jesus is promising that the kingdom of God, which dawned with his coming into the world, will arrive in its full glory at some future time. Then will prevail the biblical ideal of the peaceable community, where natural enemies become loving neighbors and unbroken fellowship with God is finally realized. The parable stresses the future dimension of this event. The kingdom is surely coming, but only God knows exactly when.

The key, Jesus insists, is to be prepared. In the parable he explains that the kingdom will come unexpectedly, like a bridegroom who arrives late for his wedding. Only those who maintain readiness—like the wise maidens who make sure they always have oil for their lamps—will be allowed to join the wedding party when the celebration finally commences.

Because the kingdom has yet to be completely installed by God, Jesus' counsel remains valid. Those who long for the coming kingdom, as does any Christian when she prays the Lord's Prayer, must always be ready for its arrival. How does one do so? Not by engaging in wild speculation about the date, location, and circumstances of the end times, as do self-anointed "prophets" who claim to have all the answers about the mysteries of faith. Because of the human desire for certainty, many are attracted to these seers, but their rantings are void because they are unbiblical. If the Son of God himself could not provide such answers, what human being dares do so?

Rather, we prepare by devoting ourselves here and now to the life of the Church, the body of Christ. God instituted that community through Jesus and sustains it by the Holy Spirit, so that the believer may have a way station in this world while awaiting the world to come. The Church fulfills this mission by keeping alive the sacred memory of God's saving activity, without which the world would plunge into despair, by practicing the values of the kingdom, as taught and applied by Jesus; by functioning as a fellowship of suffering and service for those on the pilgrimage from this world to the next; and by proclaiming the good news of God's kingdom, present and future, that all might hear and respond.

In sum, the Christian prepares for the coming kingdom by attending to the present, ongoing life of the Church. This may not be as splashy as predicting the particulars of Armageddon, but it is in keeping with the biblical truth, and that's what counts.

I never thought about all this when I played golf with my women friends at Trinity, but in retrospect it occurs to me that they were "wise maidens" on the course. May they be examples for us Christians as we live out the everyday life of faith in the Church, so that when the kingdom comes, we'll be ready.

6

Shotmaking

"For which of you, intending to
build a tower, does not first
sit down and estimate the
cost, to see whether he has
enough to complete it?"

Luke 14:28

Shotmaking

A TREE IS 85 percent air." No, that's not the scientific calculation of a botanist. It is reputed to be a statement Jack Nicklaus once made about trouble shots in golf, a counsel of boldness for golfers confronted by obstacles like a towering oak blocking the ball's flight path to the green.

Easy for him to say. Over the years the Golden Bear has circumvented thousands of trees, traps, bogs, and ponds, but then he can knock the ball down, over, or around trouble on demand. What happens when we amateurs attempt the same magic?

Most often, it backfires, at least in my experience. The par I would save by punching a low hook through the foot-wide corridor between two massive pines turns into a triple bogey when the ball clunks off one of the trees into a bush, leaving me an unplayable lie two hundred yards from the hole. I can almost count on one hand the times I've successfully negotiated such a shot.

Once I figured out I'm no Jack Nicklaus, I began to have fewer of these disasters. Oh, I still get into trouble; I've just learned, as my daddy used to say, "to play the percentages," to focus on getting the ball back in play instead of trying to be a hero. While this does reduce the possibility of spectacular saves, it also shrinks the debacle quota. It's a good trade.

The lesson we may abstract from this aspect of the game is to carefully size up our options. Wisdom dictates that before we act impetuously, especially where some risk is involved, we count the cost to get some idea of the consequences we face if our effort doesn't pan out. This doesn't eliminate the possibility of our choosing the bold alternative—it just helps us decide responsibly by preparing us to live with its aftermath.

This solid, everyday wisdom applies to all aspects of life, as shown in Jesus' saying about building a tower. Here he teaches that nothing can be accomplished without commitment, and no genuine commitment can be reached without clear vision as to the cost involved. Jesus illustrates the point with an example from the construction trade. No successful builder would erect a tower without first making careful projections of the quantity and cost of materials necessary for the project's timely completion. To do otherwise would be foolish. Who would hire a builder with a record of unfinished projects and cost overruns?

The same truth applies to the decisions people make about Jesus. He wants them to believe in him and follow his way, but he also wants them to see what they're getting themselves into from the outset of their relationship with him. To appreciate his mighty works and marvel at his teachings from a distance is not sufficient ground for deciding to follow him. Potential disciples must know up front that commitment to Jesus—true commitment—requires placing him above all else, even though sacrifice may be in the offing. Any doubt about this is dispelled by the two conditions with which Jesus brackets the tower saying: "Whoever comes to me and does not hate father and mother, wife and children, brothers and sisters, yes, and even life itself, cannot be my disciple" (Luke 14:26), and "So therefore, none of you can become my disciple if you do not give up all your possessions" (Luke 14:33).

Jesus wants us to recognize the high cost of discipleship before we make our decision. He doesn't want fairweather Christians who admire him when things go well but disappear when confronted by the harsh consequences his disciples inevitably face. If we commit, we need to know exactly what we're committing to: entering into solidarity with those who suffer, as Jesus did; asserting the principles of God's kingdom over the world's values, as Jesus did; pursuing the truth, even when it flies in the face of our own religious institutions, as Jesus did; trusting more in God's care for us than in our care for ourselves, as Jesus did; and understanding "family" in terms other than blood and legal kinship, as Jesus did.

It is a high cost. What keeps it in perspective is the price God paid to make salvation available to us—the suffering and death of Jesus, God's own child. This amazing action redeems the world. We avail ourselves of its benefits by making our commitment to God through Christ. To do so is costly, but never so expensive as the commitment God has made to us.

Interestingly, this may be one of those places where golf and faith diverge. Both call for assessing consequences before we act. In golf this usually steers most of us toward the more conservative option. In faith the process must result in the radical response of following God by becoming disciples of Jesus Christ. The one move is relatively safe, the other decidedly bold. Either requires counting the cost, which we must do if we are to make the decisive effort called for by both golf and faith.

7

Welcome Back, Zinger

". . . we also boast in our
sufferings, knowing that
suffering produces endurance,
and endurance produces
character, and character
produces hope, and hope
does not disappoint us . . ."
Romans 5:3–5

Welcome Back,
Zinger

I'VE WATCHED many a televised golf tournament in
my day, but none more memorable than the "Wendy's
Three-Tour Challenge" match aired near the end of the
1993 season. This format sets up a competition among
players representing the women's, men's, and senior
men's tours. It happened that Raymond Floyd shot a
course record round to lead the seniors to victory in
this inaugural playing of the event, but that was not its
highlight as far as I'm concerned.

When Paul Azinger, a member of the men's team,
was preparing to finish on the eighteenth green, a precious little girl probably no more than two years old
managed to escape her mother and toddle out to him
as he was surveying his putt. Rather than back off with
a scowl at such a distraction, Paul gleefully scooped the

child up in his arms and made her his playing partner for that moment. Together they sashayed around the green, checking its contour and examining the cup. Returning to the ball, Paul wrapped her tiny fingers around the putter shaft and helped her poke the ball toward the hole. He then convulsed with laughter—as did the surrounding gallery—when she picked up the ball, hovered unsteadily over the cup, and, after several false starts, dropped it into the hole. The crowd could not have roared louder for a hole-in-one.

That the telecast was shown tape-delayed instead of live made this scene all the more touching, since many of the viewers were aware of the news, broken a few days prior to the airing of the tournament, that Azinger had been diagnosed with cancer. We can rejoice now that because of early detection and effective treatment, he has completely recovered. But at the outset the news stunned—not just that one so young and strong had been attacked by physical affliction, but that one so obviously decent would be victimized by tragedy. Why is it this way? Why do bad things happen to good people?

As a minister, I've been confronted with this question on some painful occasions. There's no good answer that lays the question to rest, but I know a bad answer that attempts to do so: "It was God's will." I realize that people who offer this explanation in the midst of tragedy often do so out of compassion, their implicit reasoning being that any answer is better than none at all. But this answer is dead wrong. It implies that absolutely nothing happens without God's direct involvement, which contradicts the biblical understanding of Creation; moreover, it makes God the author of random evil, which flies in the face of the biblical witness to God's loving nature.

What, then, can be said? On a rational level we can consider a couple of possibilities. Sometimes bad occurrences are the consequences of bad choices people make, as with the addict who loses everything on account of her addiction. Sometimes bad consequences are imposed upon an innocent bystander, as when the pedestrian is killed by a drunk driver. In both cases there is the element of human accountability; tragedy occurs because someone's actions, intentional or not, make it inevitable.

Then there are those happenings—like a killer hurricane—whose reason for being we cannot fathom. Meteorologists can provide a scientific analysis of this phenomenon, but nobody can say how it fits in the grand scheme of things. Insofar as we can tell, such events are not the consequences of human sin; rather they are random evil, remnants, perhaps, of the chaos that preceded Creation.

But these explanations, true as they may be, provide

little initial comfort for those who must cope with the suffering that bad times bring. Fortunately, the Christian faith does not stop here. While Christianity promises its followers no exemption from suffering, it does assure them that they never suffer alone. The image of the crucified Christ serves as an indestructible reminder of the depth of God's compassionate commitment to accompany us in all circumstances, especially in those where our pain is greatest.

Otherwise, the apostle Paul's exhortation to boast in suffering is madness. How can he so boldly assert that suffering leads to good (endurance, character, and hope)? Because he knows from personal experience that while Christ is everywhere, he is especially in the midst of suffering, and wherever Christ is, good cannot fail to be. This means that Christ doesn't just help us endure the bad times—Christ redeems them. While that may not silence the question about why bad things happen to good people, it does rob the question of its power to bedevil us.

I have only a fan's knowledge of Paul Azinger, but if the interview following his victory in the '93 PGA tournament, not long before his cancer diagnosis, is any indication, he knows what I'm talking about. Then he unabashedly thanked God for seeing him through that critical moment in his career. I suspect he's since discovered that that experience of God's presence at a high point in his life pales in comparison with how he felt God's power during his recent season of suffering.

He's returned to the tour now, playing his way back into competitive shape. A popular player before he left, he's even more so now. Folks still want to see his golfing artistry, but they also want to tap into that quality that shone through his battle with adversity. That quality is faith.

Welcome back, Zinger, and thanks.

8

The Greatest
Lesson

". . . Do this in remembrance
of me."
1 Corinthians 11:24

The Greatest
Lesson

Even THE greatest touring pros occasionally need help to diagnose and cure an ailing swing. Some turn to fellow players or to a retired golfing legend. Many, however, consult with teachers from their formative years, golf professionals who may be virtually unknown to the public. Jack Nicklaus, for example, would go back to his early teacher, the late Jack Grout, for consultation on his swing. Grout never made a big name for himself as a tournament player; what notoriety he received as a professional golfer came primarily from his being Jack Nicklaus's teacher. This implies that one need not be a great player in order to be an excellent teacher. But whatever his background, a pro does not build a reputation as a master teacher unless he is blessed with certain gifts. For example, he must inspire confidence, especially if he suggests major changes in a golfer's swing. Unless he can persuade his pupil that such radical "surgery" is worth the risk and effort, the new approach will have no chance. He will also need to be a clear communicator. Most important, he has to be a perceptive analyst with the ability to break down a swing, spot the problem, and offer an imaginative approach to correcting it.

The importance of the last skill cannot be overemphasized. Many golfers, even amateurs, are capable swing diagnosticians; they know enough about fundamentals to identify major flaws. The real trick is to propose a remedy that both makes sense to the pupil and promises to be a change he can readily incorporate into his swing. The object is to convert a bad habit into a good one, which requires suggesting just the right cue to help this particular golfer make the transition. Many golfers can spot a flying elbow, a reverse pivot, or a too-strong grip a mile away, but how many know what to say to deliver their pupil from such errors? This gift separates the master teacher from the hack.

Jesus certainly qualifies as a master teacher in this respect. He knows people's problems and the kind of language that best addresses them, creating just the right cure to turn them away from sin and toward new life in God.

According to Paul's testimony, perhaps the greatest

example of this kind of cue is Jesus' institution of the Lord's Supper. We call this a sacrament, but we can think of it as a "holy cue." Because it symbolizes Jesus' sacrificial offering of himself, it reminds us of our flawed nature, which necessitated God's taking such drastic action on our behalf. Partaking of Communion thus helps us remember both the problem—our sinfulness—and the solution—God's forgiving grace made available through Jesus' suffering, death, and resurrection. It promises that we don't have to remain trapped in a bad pattern but can, through faith, live a new life.

All Christians need to stay in touch with this important cue, for sin is more than an abstract concept we only discuss in Sunday school or hear in a sermon. It is a grim, oppressive reality forever invading our daily existence. We wrestle with it on the job, in school, at home. Whether we are sin's victim or its perpetrator, we never fully escape it. Unbridled lust for things, selfish manipulation of relationships, reckless disregard for truth, callous insensitivity to others' suffering—these are the fruits of sin. We may be growing them unaware, or we may have developed a facility for pretending they don't exist. In either case, the scales are bound to fall off our eyes eventually, and we'll see things aren't right.

Then, like the golfer whose game is on the skids, we look for one who can help us. If we seek Jesus and place ourselves in his care, we discover why his contemporaries referred to him as both Master and Teacher. He inspires, he communicates, he diagnoses, and best of all he cues us, providing reminders that set us in the right direction. His cues are rich and varied, everything from biblical stories and teachings to the symbols that have come to adorn his Church. None is more powerful than the sacrament he initiated at his last meal with the disciples. When we participate in it, we remember that God forgives us our sins, which frees us to move toward a new life as redeemed people.

As a pastor, I have puzzled over why some Christians seem to be put off by Communion. Such an attitude can be traced to any number of reasons, including plain old misunderstanding. The sacrament will always be mysterious, but it should never create misunderstanding. It may help those who struggle with it to think of Communion as a teaching occasion, not unlike when a master teaching pro helps a frustrated golfer untangle his swing. Jesus is that pro for you and me, and the Lord's Table is the practice tee. The bread and wine we receive there remind us, as nothing else can, of what's basic—the unconditional love of God, which will not let us go. If ever there was a holy cue to set our lives straight, this is it.

9

Etiquette

"Mary took a pound of costly
perfume made of pure nard,
anointed Jesus' feet, and
wiped them with her hair."
John 12:3

Etiquette

MY FATHER, who laid the foundation for my love of the game, played what he called "sociable golf." While it does not discount the competitive aspect, sociable golf does set the competition in the context of fellowship. For my dad and his golfing buddies, it was most important to enjoy one another's company, regardless of who won the match on any given Saturday. The teams, therefore, were always relatively even in skill, the wagers small, and the negotiating terms generous. On the occasions I caddied, I can't remember anyone getting bent out of shape because of the way a match was conducted or concluded. That pleasant exposure undoubtedly pulled me toward the game.

An important part of sociable golf is "golf etiquette," the code of sportsmanship civilized golfers practice on the course. While it has nothing to do with the proper execution of the swing, golf etiquette has everything to do with respecting those who are concentrating on trying to make that swing. Keeping quiet and avoiding movement when another player's away, not hitting out of turn, tending the flag, letting a faster group play through—such courtesies constitute golf etiquette, the practice of which makes the game more enjoyable for all.

So I've come to believe that being a complete golfer is more than just knowing swing mechanics and the rule book. It also involves practicing golf etiquette. Not everyone agrees with me, though; at least, that's what I conclude by the golfers I encounter now and then who show little awareness of this relational aspect of the game.

Why are people this way? Often they simply don't know any better; they haven't played the game long enough or haven't had anyone teach them proper course behavior. If one can intervene without being self-righteous or overbearing—ideally through modeling— it's possible to help these people become more complete and winsome golfers.

Unless, of course, they are hard cases, people who have played long enough and at a high enough level to know better, but who nevertheless refuse to observe golf etiquette. They seem to be loners in a social game. I don't pretend to know why this is; I merely observe that these golfers get so wrapped up in themselves that they become oblivious to those around them. They're so intent on their own shots that they play out of turn; they're so determined to read the green that they stalk it while someone else is trying to putt; they're so worried about losing a stroke that they refuse to give up on their lost ball, even as the course is stacking up behind them. It may be argued that some of these people possess the gift of intense concentration, which can be a boon; however, when one player's concentration tramples on his neighbors' opportunity to focus on their own efforts, concentration becomes self-centeredness. Only a healthy dose of golf etiquette can cure this condition.

Sometimes we misconstrue the practice of the Christian faith in a similar way. Keen to its demand that we live an obedient life, we grow intense about piling up deeds to document our good works. In the extreme, such Christianity becomes cold and calculating, a strictly bottom-line operation. In this mode we may do many good things—teach Sunday school, give money, sing in the choir, carry a meal to a grieving family—but in a joyless, wooden way. We focus so intently on our performance that we fail to connect meaningfully with those we would serve; worse, we lose touch with the Christ whose message, if we took it to heart, would free us from the compulsion so that we might be truly with and for others.

When just before his death Mary bathes Jesus' feet with expensive ointment, she acts extravagantly; some would say irresponsibly. Of all the good things she could have done, such as selling the precious nard and giving the proceeds to the poor, Mary chooses to anoint Jesus. Rather than chastise her for being silly and wasteful, Jesus blesses her for this. By attending to the common courtesy of washing a guest's feet, and doing so in such a caring way, Mary offers love, a gift worth far more than the expensive ointment itself. By affirming this act Jesus demonstrates that the defining characteristic of obedience is love. This may be enacted in everyday expressions of hospitality as well as in monumental deeds of justice. Whatever its scale, if an act is to constitute genuine Christian obedience, it must express love.

To be a complete golfer, we must practice golf etiquette. Likewise, to be a complete Christian, we must love in all situations, small and large. This is the kind of obedience God in Jesus Christ calls out of us. It grants no license to equate Christianity with mere politeness, proper manners, or good taste. But neither will it let us forget that it is always appropriate to love, no matter how inconsequential the circumstances might seem.

10

The More You
Practice, the
Luckier You Get

". . . Train yourself in godliness,
for, while physical training
is of some value, godliness
is valuable in every way."
1 Timothy 4:7–8

The More You Practice, the Luckier You Get

UPON WINNING a golf tournament, Raymond Floyd was asked what role luck played in his victory. The interviewer believed that Raymond had benefited from a good break on a critical shot coming down the stretch, and he wanted to draw out the story of that turning point. Professional golfers normally comply with such a request by recalling the moment in detail, usually confirming the interviewer's assumption. But not Raymond, not this time.

Instead, with a hint of indignation he launched into a reflection on his early years on the pro tour. He admitted that in those days he pretty much got by on his raw athletic talent. He also confessed that like his great golfing forebear, Walter Hagen, he loved the good life and had no intention of letting golf infringe upon the full enjoyment of his salad days. Besides, he was making a good living from a relatively small expenditure of effort. Why spoil a good thing?

That attitude changed after he got married, he related. The stability of the new relationship did not suddenly turn him into a wallflower, but it did give him a different perspective on life as a whole, including his profession. He realized he was only scratching the surface of his gift. He had been a good professional golfer at virtually no personal cost. What might happen, he began to wonder, if he dedicated himself to developing his golfing potential?

For the first time in his career he committed to working on his golf. He practiced in earnest, raising the level of his game both physically and mentally. In so doing he gained an important insight, with which he concluded the interview. Looking his interrogator straight in the eye, he proclaimed, "And the moral of the story is, the more you practice, the luckier you get."

Clearly, Raymond was steamed over the insinuation that his victory had been a fluke. But would he actually deny that luck sometimes does affect, one way or another, the outcome of a round? I doubt it. In a cooler moment Raymond would probably concede that luck does occasionally intervene on the course. Nonetheless, his point stands; in order to be in position to take advantage of a good break, or to overcome a bad one, a golfer must surround the moment with many good shots. To do so requires skill, which, while natural to a degree, can only be sharpened through hard work.

For Raymond this means making the practice area his office. For us in our Christian walk it means submitting ourselves to the disciplined life that moves a person closer to God. While faith is a gift, it is not to be received passively. Like the wise stewards in the parable of the talents, we are to take the measure of faith we receive and develop it.

This is the advice the writer of the letters to Timothy gives his protégé in ministry: "Train yourself in godliness . . ." This admonition, though addressed to one in a set-apart leadership role in an early Christian congregation, is good counsel for all who inhabit the household of faith, laity and clergy alike. We rejoice in our initial awakening to God through the gift of faith, but awakening is merely a turning point, our entry into a new way of life. God promises to accompany us in this transformation, but for us to sit back and "put it in God's hands" is not an option. Faith does not work by remote control. God grants us the freedom to decide whether or not we'll accept the invitation to live a faithful life. Either we choose to do so, and give it our best, or we don't.

If we choose to accept the invitation to faith and take full advantage of it, we must "train." Just as Raymond hits hundreds of practice shots—fades, draws, punches, explosions, pitches, chips, and putts—the believer builds faith by working at "practicing the presence of God." This involves many activities, including prayer, charity, exemplary living, and commitment to the body of Christ. We pray, because this is our way of maintaining communication with the source and end of our faith, God. We practice charity, the graceful love that is supremely exemplified in Jesus Christ, because doing so constitutes our obedience unto God. We try constantly to show ourselves good examples of being rightly related to God, thereby maintaining the integrity of our witness. We commit to a local congregation of believers, because we affirm that God's salvation comes and is sustained through an ongoing, historical community of faith.

No matter how many thousands of practice balls Raymond hits, he will never become the perfect golfer; likewise, no matter how diligently we "practice the presence of God," we will never become perfect believers. Still, when we claim our gifts and devote ourselves to the discipline of practicing them daily, our faith matures, bringing increasing joy to God and blessing to the world. Or, as Raymond Floyd might say if he were a preacher, the more we practice our faith, the more faithful we get.

11
Toward the Target

"I press on toward the goal for
the prize of the heavenly call
of God in Christ Jesus."
Philippians 3:14

Toward the Target

BECAUSE OF the generosity of family and friends, I have been able to attend the Masters golf tournament now and again. If you've been yourself, I don't need to paint a picture for you; if you haven't, I wish I commanded the descriptive power to do the experience justice. I'll just say that the Masters is to the golfer what Mecca is to the Muslim. If the opportunity ever presents itself, make the pilgrimage to Augusta!

Many patrons walk the course, following their favorite pro on his round, but I suspect the majority have a special roosting place where they settle in and let the action come to them. The strategically located bleachers and inviting mounds scattered about the course cater to those who prefer this option.

I've done both on my visits to Augusta National and

have discovered I prefer roosting. I especially like to perch on the bleachers at the main practice tee. While this position removes you from the on-course drama, it has several advantages. You're able to get relatively close to the players and often pick up snatches of their conversations. Sometimes they even banter with the crowd, which is a delightful bonus, and many will sign autographs. You get to see them hit a variety of shots as they work their way through the bag in their warm-up routine. You also get a close view of their equipment.

To me the most satisfying thing about this vantage point is that it enables you to study at close range the different swings. Generally, the whole field of players will spend time here before they tee off, and usually there are several pros hitting simultaneously, so you have an unsurpassed opportunity to compare the rich variety of styles. Over the years, for example, I've seen the molasses swing of Bob Murphy next to Lanny Wadkins's blur, the upright swing of Jack Nicklaus hard by the flat swing of Corey Pavin, and the fade of Lee Trevino bending away from the draw of Gary Player.

Regardless of the different styles, one thing remains constant: All these guys hit the ball to the target. This was especially apparent in the days when they hit to their caddies who would stand out in the range and shag the shots. It always amazed me how little a caddie had to move to pick up his man's shots, and not just when the pro had a wedge in his hand. All the way through the bag, even down to the long irons and woods, every pro consistently put the ball within a step or two of his caddie's position. Given the opportunity to warm up this way, most of us would get a caddie in shape to run a marathon, but not the pros in the Masters field.

That shouldn't surprise, though. Golf is, after all, a target-oriented game. On our drives we zero in on the optimum portion of the landing area and line up with the intention of hitting to that position. On our fairway shots we aim for the flag or, if prudence dictates otherwise, for the safe section of the green. On our short shots, we lock in on the spot we want to pitch or chip the ball to, in order to start an accurate roll toward the hole. And on our putts we aim for the cup, or some point on either side, depending on the green's contour and grain. Regardless of the kind of shot called for, the golfer must aim.

Pros do this better than anyone; that's why they're pros. So target-conscious are they that they never just flail away. Even on the practice tee, they're hitting every shot to a target. Not only does this habit enhance their physical ability to hit accurate shots; it also ingrains in them a target mentality that serves them well in the heat of competition.

Christians are called to operate with no less sense of goal-orientation, as Paul announces to the Philippians.

In Jesus Christ the world has been invited into a new relationship with God, a relationship more precious than the most intimate of human bonds. God offers the possibility of this relationship as a gift, but the believer must intentionally move toward it, establishing it as the top priority in his life.

How does one do this? Referring to his own experience, Paul says that a critical first step is to become liberated from one's past in order to focus on the target of ultimate reconciliation with God, which lies in the future. In Paul's case this meant pulling away from the law, on which he had staked everything—no small sacrifice for a rabbi. Through Christ he learned that one's future with God depends on God's gift of grace accepted in faith, not on one's mastery of the law, no matter how prodigious. Indeed, Paul's infatuation with the law had diverted his eyes from the real prize of reconciliation with God. It took a traumatic encounter with Jesus to get him focused on the only true goal, "the prize of the heavenly call of God in Christ Jesus."

This doesn't necessarily mean that a Damascus road experience awaits each of us; nevertheless, we need to assume a stance similar to Paul's, aiming for the same target. We cannot be satisfied with a vague sense of "just getting by." Whatever blocks us from the core purpose of our faith—reconciliation with God and God's world by

God's grace—must be removed so that we zero in on the target clearly and do our best to hit it.

There's no such thing as aimless Christianity. It always involves living toward the goal of reconciliation with God and the world through Jesus Christ. This is a concept that golfers especially should have no trouble grasping because of their target-consciousness. Our efforts in faith may not always "rattle the pin," but we know that's the ideal, and we proceed accordingly. Fortunately, where our own skill is inadequate, God's grace takes control and gives us the Master's accuracy. On that we can depend, so long as we're trying to hit the target.

12

Sticking to
the Basics

"You shall love the Lord your
God . . . and . . . your neighbor
as yourself. There is no other
commandment greater
than these."
Mark 12:30–31

Sticking to
the Basics

FOR A golfer the Holy Grail is a consistent golf swing, one that automatically and faithfully repeats itself without undue thinking, especially when the pressure is on. This separates the topflight professionals from all other golfers; they can count on their swings to hold up, even when a fortune hangs in the balance.

How is this level of consistency reached? Take one large measure of natural ability, add hundreds of hours of practice, and season with occasional advice from a wise observer/teacher who can correct and refine the swing. Finally, simplify things by building the swing around a few basic principles. This will make it easier to maintain and manage, which is critical when the heat's on.

Curtis Strange testified to this after winning his second consecutive U.S. Open. Asked how he handled the pressure of the final nine holes, he replied that he simply concentrated on the basics, going on to explain that for him this means focusing on the work of the big muscles to produce a sound swing. If the legs, back, shoulders, and arms do what they're supposed to do, the hands and feet will come along for the ride.

Would Strange's "big muscle" theory work for us? Maybe, but that's not really my point. Listen to any number of champions reflect on their success, and you'll hear a variety of explanations about what makes for a pressure-proof swing. One element, however, pops up again and again—simplicity. Great golfers turn to whatever makes up their bedrock basics when they're standing on Augusta National's eighteenth tee with a one-stroke lead in the final round of the Masters. So must we, if we want to have a trustworthy swing.

This wisdom applies to many aspects of life, including how we understand and practice our religion. It speaks to those who desire fervently to be the kind of people God wants them to be. Sometimes their zeal turns into compulsion, drowning them in trivialities. When the basics are thus obscured, it becomes all but impossible to fulfill the desire to please God.

The Bible diagnoses and treats this problem. At the

outset of the biblical narrative, God, dealing with Abraham, lays an elegantly simple foundation for establishing the proper relationship between Creator and Creation. The building material for this foundation is love. God promises to love and provide for the Creation, which is expected in return to love God above everything and to allow love to rule all human relationships. Later, God does some finish work on the foundation by introducing the Ten Commandments, broad principles that clarify the shape that love of God and one's neighbors is to take.

Though God deemed this understanding sufficient, the covenant people did not. For basically well-intentioned but ultimately misguided reasons, they overlaid God's simple foundation with hundreds of "statutes and ordinances," rules and regulations which try to anticipate every possible situation and provide a ready-made "right" response for it. On top of this was plastered the "traditions of the elders," an expansive oral commentary on the written code, which was considered by many to carry the same weight as Scripture itself. As a result, the system grew into such a large, tangled nest of do's, don't's, and multiple interpretations that the essence of the covenant relationship with God—love for God and neighbor—was all but obscured.

Against this background Jesus answered the scribe's question about the heart of the law. "Love God and neighbor" is more than a handy summary of the faith, suitable for needlepointing. It is the Messiah's pleading with the chosen people to return to the basics they had forgotten over time. Jesus' pleading offended because the people preferred their own fabrication, complicated though it was, to his call for a return to essentials. So they killed him. Only after the Resurrection did it become clear that even hearts so hard as theirs could not resist God's insistence on the essentials. God wants love, nothing more, nothing less. Jesus' crucifixion and resurrection are the ultimate confirmation of this.

So when we find ourselves puzzling over how to keep faith with God, we need only get in touch with the basics—love God and neighbor. Granted, it takes effort on our part to figure out how that love should be expressed in the particular circumstances in which we find ourselves in any given moment. God holds us responsible for making and acting upon those kinds of interpretations, but there's never any doubt about the guiding principle of the process—it is love.

We may never stand on number eighteen at Augusta National with a chance to win the Masters, but we will all face crucial situations in our lives. Isn't it good to know we need not be strung out by needless complications at those crunch times? God has given us the simple, basic key—love. If we will only trust it and let it do its work, we'll win a reward far greater than the green jacket.

13

Trusting the Stroke

"Now faith is the assurance
of things hoped for, the
conviction of things not seen."
Hebrews 11:1

Trusting the Stroke

I NEVER PLAYED with a better putter than Henry. Though I constantly outdrove him and played comparable fairway shots with shorter irons, he beat me like a drum. Many times I smugly admired my ball on the green while he was yet a pitch away, only to self-destruct with a three-putt while he got up and down for a win.

Finally, I could take it no more. Throwing myself on Henry's mercy, I begged him to teach me the secret of his putting artistry. He took pity and agreed to a tutoring session on the practice green.

He began with the truism that "putting is 95 percent mental, a matter of confidence." Not wishing to offend my mentor, I listened respectfully until an opening presented itself. "But Henry," I finally protested, "a guy's gotta make a putt occasionally to build some confidence. How do I sink that first one? Talk mechanics to me."

"Okay," he said testily, as if to chasten me for my impatience. "Watch this and tell me what you see." Dropping three balls about ten feet from the hole, he proceeded to make two of the three putts, lipping out the third.

At once it came to me. How I missed it during our rounds on the course, I don't know. For whatever reasons, it came clear that moment. "You don't look up, even after you stroke the ball," I blurted. "Your head stays perfectly still."

"Eureka!" he shouted sarcastically. "You don't watch the ball go into the hole; you hear it. That way you know you've kept your head down and steady, which is the key. It takes confidence and discipline to putt like this; you won't master it overnight. But it works. End of lesson. Now, how about going over to the practice tee and helping me squeeze ten more yards out of my driver?"

Though I never became anywhere near as good a putter as Henry, I did get better (hard not to, when you've got nowhere to go but up). Far more important, that episode illumined my understanding of faith in a way no book, lecture, or sermon ever did. According to the writer of Hebrews, faith, like Henry's putting, is a matter of confidence and discipline. It is "the assurance of things hoped for." The faithful Christian lives with confidence because he constantly receives assurance through the Bible, the Church, and the Holy Spirit that God never stops loving Creation. When beset by suffering, we easily lose sight of this promise because God's love appears to be hidden. That's when faith kicks in, reminding us that no matter how bad the present seems, the future, which is in God's hands, is already determined to be blessed. Such a conviction sustained Abraham on the road to Mt. Moriah, Joseph in the Egyptian jail, Moses by the Red Sea, David against Goliath, and Jesus on the cross. It promises to sustain you and me too. Just as Henry approaches every putt feeling he can make it, the believer exudes confidence, even in trying times, because he never loses hope in the ultimate victory of God's goodness.

But faith is also "the conviction of things not seen," which is where Henry's putting technique is especially illustrative. As simple as Henry's counsel sounds—keep your head so steady that you hear the ball, rather than see it, go into the hole—it's hard to do. Our natural tendency is to look up as soon as the putt has been struck (sometimes sooner!) to watch it roll toward the cup. Often this yips our stroke, causing us to push or pull the ball off the proper line. We know that keeping the head steady is a cardinal rule, yet we're tempted to peek, which ruins our effort. Discipline!

It's the same with faith. To be a Christian is to live a life of obedience to the will of God as revealed in Jesus Christ. This means to love God and neighbor in such a way that the kingdom of this world comes into closer conformity with the kingdom of God. That is the Christian's goal, the ideal that he is bound to pursue.

If we attack this goal in an undisciplined manner— if we don't keep our head steady over the ball—we won't make much progress toward it. As with putting, it's an easy error to fall into. Sometimes doubt creeps in; we know what being a true Christian requires, but because we doubt whether it's really possible, we tend to be skittish.

We miss the mark because we forget that God is our guiding companion in the attempt to live a faithful life. Sure, we're expected to do our part. Just as Henry studies the grain, reads the break, and calculates the speed of the green, so the believer must prepare to live out obedience. But once Henry has done all he can to get ready, he locks in on the ball and strokes away, trusting in a positive result. The believer must do the same.

Once the Christian does all he can to prepare, he attempts obedience, not worrying about the outcome but trusting God to enable all things to work for the good. While this doesn't guarantee what he might consider the perfect outcome in every situation, faith does promise that whatever the result of his actions, if he has undertaken them so as to love God and neighbor, God will bring them to some good conclusion. This is "the conviction of things not seen."

It works—but only if you keep the head down and trust the stroke.

14

You Are How
You Play

"And now do not be distressed,
or angry with yourselves,
because you sold me here;
for God sent me before
you to preserve life."

Genesis 45:5

You Are How
You Play

YOU CAN tell a lot about a person, even a total stranger, by playing a round of golf with him. Obviously, you note physical characteristics—how strong and supple, how deliberate or quick he is. But watch how he handles the problems and opportunities the round presents, and you gain insight into interior qualities, such as his temperament, ethic, judgment, and sense of relationship. To be sure, a round of golf doesn't constitute psychoanalysis, but it does reveal much about how the player lives his life as a whole. In short, you get a reading into his character.

Does he have a ready excuse for every missed shot (his ailing back, the clatter of a nearby cart, a poorly cut cup)? Is he oblivious to his playing partners, constantly hitting out of turn? Is he a "psych artist," offering a not-so-subtle running commentary on your swing? Is he begrudging of any good shot you play? Does he get so upset when the group ahead plays too slowly, or the group behind pushes too hard, that his complaining spoils the round for his own group? If you ever have to play with someone like that, chances are you never will again if you can help it. Moreover, your experience on the golf course likely kills any desire to relate to him professionally, socially, or any other way.

Fortunately, this scenario is, within my experience, uncommon. Since virtually all my golf is of the public course "pick-up" variety, I often play with strangers. Seldom have I had a round that was more an endurance test than a pleasure. While most golfers exhibit a peculiarity or two, only rarely is one totally obnoxious. Somehow, those folks don't last very long in golf, or else they play a lot of solitary rounds.

Indeed, most of my golfing acquaintances prove to be quite pleasant, and some are downright inspiring. Take Joe, for example. At first I thought he was a Doug Sanders disciple, so short and abrupt was his swing. After the usual icebreaking small talk, I couldn't help but inquire about how he developed his technique. Had he patterned it after Sanders?

He chuckled good-naturedly, as if to let me know I wasn't the first to be curious. Then he proceeded to tell me the story behind the swing. In his late teens he had possessed a long, flowing, powerful swing, the result of good golf genes and a lot of hard work on the practice tee. About the time he had his handicap down to a two, he was drafted into the Army, underwent infantry training, and shipped out to Vietnam. In his first combat experience he was wounded. Though his account was spare, I did learn that in addition to taking shrapnel, he suffered shattered bone and torn muscle which, though repaired surgically, could not be completely restored. The result was limited range of motion in his upper torso; hence the swing that would fit in a telephone booth.

Feeling pity, I attempted to express my sorrow at his cruel fate, but he would have none of it. "Actually," he said, "I feel like I'm the luckiest guy in the world still to be able to play. Besides, that big limberback swing I had when I was a kid was bound to get me in trouble sooner or later. With the small swing I've got now, there's not much that can go wrong, and even if it does, the mistake won't be so exaggerated as it used to be when I took a big cut."

What an honor to play with Joe, not on account of the beauty of his game but because of the strength of his character. He reminds me of another Joe—Joseph, the son of Jacob, one of the Bible's most marvelous exemplars of character. Sold into slavery by his own brothers, then jailed through the treachery of his Egyptian master's wife, Joseph has reason to believe that the world is against him, that there is no justice anywhere. Instead, he trusts that his present sufferings are not in vain, that some good purpose will eventually be served for his having lived through them. He doesn't complain about his hard times; he looks for the good that can come out of them. Later, after those days of hardship leave him in a position to preserve his family, his attitude is confirmed. "What you meant as harm to me, God turned into good for us," Joseph tells his brothers when he reveals himself to them. They have difficulty seeing things this way, but not Joseph. He always looks for God's providential hand at work, even in the midst of trouble.

Isn't that what character is all about—exploring our troubled circumstances for what's good, what's possible, what's redemptive? Life presents many such opportunities. When illness or injury strikes, when important relationships are tested, when tough decisions are demanded, when sense of purpose flickers—on such occasions we have a choice. We can succumb to bitter self-pity, or we can resolve to become stronger through the adversity.

To assume the positive stance takes character; it also builds character. When we face a tough choice, it helps to realize we're not alone. We take courage in those moments by remembering the "Joe's" we've met in our lives, whether on the first tee or in Holy Scripture. They show us the difference between whining and winning. They inspire us to do the same for someone else.

Yes, you can learn a lot about a person's character by observing him at golf. What conclusions does your game suggest to those who play with you?

15

Willing the Shot

". . . for now I know that you
fear God, since you have
not withheld your son,
your only son, from me."
Genesis 22:12

Willing the Shot

THOUGH I was hooked on golf in the early 1960s, my first hero was not Palmer, Player, or Nicklaus. I favored Bobby Locke, the South African whose career by then was beginning to wind down. I suppose I was captivated because the first golf show I ever watched was Jimmy Demaret's *All Star Golf.* Televised weekly, its format was an eighteen-hole match between two "name" pros, the winner returning for subsequent matches until he was finally defeated. I saw a lot of Locke because he ran up the longest victory string of any of Demaret's guests.

I remember Locke for his courtly manner, his plus fours and tie, his sweeping hook, and his mallet-head putter. Mostly, though, I remember him for his wedge. Besides being a magician with it on routine shots, he would use it in every other conceivable circumstance from about a hundred yards in. Whereas conventional wisdom dictates playing a variety of clubs for different shots around the green—for example, a knockdown eight-iron for a punch into the wind or a nipped five-iron for a long bump-and-run—Locke did it all with his wedge, and if he ever failed to put the ball close to the hole, it was news. *All Star Golf* became *The Bobby Locke Show* because of his prowess with that club.

Over the years I've pondered Locke's unorthodox, yet sublime, short game. How did he become the wizard of the wedge? I can only speculate that, for his own reasons, Locke developed that style at the outset of his golfing life. Perhaps it had to do with the conditions under which he learned the game, the equipment that was available to him at the time, the influence of an early teacher, or some element of personal preference. Whatever the case, the wedge became an extension of his body, resulting in one of the greatest wedge players ever.

Locke's ability to choose a particular style of play and commit himself to it unwaveringly illustrates an important dynamic of the Christian faith. The Danish theologian Kierkegaard called it "purity of heart," meaning the ability to lay everything else aside in order "to will one thing." The Bible refers to it as loving God with our total being: heart, soul, mind, and strength. It is the essence of faith.

Though no human being is able to sustain this level of faith perfectly, numerous biblical characters fulfill it episodically. There is no more dramatic instance, apart from the life of Jesus, than the story of Abraham and Isaac. As a test of faith, God commands Abraham to sacrifice Isaac, his and Sarah's only son, the seed for God's promised covenant people.

The account tells us nothing of Abraham's emotional and mental state after receiving the command, but one can imagine that both brain and heart were assaulted by troubling questions: Is this really from God, or is it just a bad dream? Why would God have me sacrifice the gift so recently given? What will become of the covenant promise of a great nation? What right have I to deprive Sarah of the joy of her life? What will I appear to be in the world's eyes? What use is my life if I should kill my son? Under such doubt Abraham likely wavered, conjuring up and weighing every possible response short of full compliance.

In the end Abraham obeyed. Sweeping away uncertainty, he took all the steps necessary to comply with God's command, his pain and bewilderment notwithstanding. Only as the knife flashed above the boy's bound body did God relent, sparing Abraham from the horrific requirement.

Later biblical authors return to the example of Abraham from time to time to flesh out the meaning of the righteousness of God which comes through faith. Far more effectively than some abstract discussion, the story of Abraham shows the direction that faith is meant to establish. It is the direction of commitment, the giving of ourselves to a particular relationship and course of action despite all the easier possibilities that tempt us. It comes from being willing to obey God, whatever the circumstances.

We don't expect to find ourselves in Abraham's position, where faith demands the ultimate sacrifice. Nevertheless, Abraham will never cease to be a model for us because faith today, as ever, requires the strongest commitment we can make to obeying God's will in real-life situations. It may call us to change our stewardship over the resources that are available to us, to rededicate ourselves to relationships that have become burdensome, to relinquish a harmful indulgence, or to strengthen our professional morality. Such transformations are demanding. As we confront them, we will wrestle with dissenting voices offering watered-down alternatives. Only our commitment to obey the will of God will keep us from opting for the easy way out.

Locke's example is instructive at this point, but Abraham's is decisive. To be our best demands single-minded commitment to will one thing. Where the life of faith is concerned, there's no better example than Abraham.

16

A Stroke
Is a Stroke

"A poor widow came and put
in two small copper coins,
which are worth a penny. Then
he called his disciples and said
to them, '. . . this poor widow
has put in more than all
those who are contributing
to the treasury.'"
Mark 12:42–43

A Stroke
Is a Stroke

IN THE strict economy of golf, each stroke counts exactly the same. It doesn't matter that athletically and aesthetically a 280-yard drive that carves the heart out of a narrow fairway bordered by hazards constitutes a far greater achievement than a six-inch putt. On the scorecard—the same!

Some of the game's best-known bromides root in this uncompromising reality. For example, "It's not how you drive but how you arrive," and "Drive for show, putt for dough." The point is, unless one develops a sound short game to complement the full shots, one will never excel at golf. This truth has haunted me my entire golfing life, as it has all golfers who have boomed many more beautiful drives than they have sunk knee-knocking putts.

As I grow older, I'm feeling a little better about the fact that golf reckons things this way. My swing's power is diminishing; consequently, I've finally started the effort to shore up my game from the other end, concentrating on the short strokes more than I ever did in the past. I'm discovering that an accurate chip and a holed three-footer have a beauty all their own. They may not be as majestic as the soaring draw that cuts the dogleg and lands in position "A," but they count the same where it matters—on the scorecard.

A similar economy obtains in the relationship between God and human beings, as the Gospel story of the widow's mite shows. On a visit to the temple Jesus observes the worshipers making their offerings. Calling the disciples to him, he points out a poor woman who places the embarrassingly small sum of one penny into the collection. Compared to the large amounts many others are contributing, hers seems insignificant—yet Jesus declares her gift superior. The wealthy people can easily spare their large contributions, but her penny represents virtually all she has. That's why Jesus lauds it above all others.

We ought not take this story as an invitation to cut back our financial support for God's work in the world. On the contrary, it invites us to contribute not in a token way, but to the fullest extent of our ability. Whatever the amount is irrelevant; to God a penny can be as extravagant as a million dollars, depending on the giver's capacity and spirit.

This is somewhat unsettling, for we live in a quantitatively oriented culture that emphasizes "the bottom line." Gross domestic product, Dow-Jones average, box-office take, championship-fight purse, salary package—our lives seem determined by the numbers. Big is good, bigger is better, small is lousy.

This mode of thinking even pervades the practice of our faith. Some believe there can be no valid expression of Christianity without benefit of multimillion dollar physical plants, six-figure ministerial salaries, and media empires. They operate with the notion that God only accepts the lavish and costly. Maybe it's this way in the business world and high society, but not where God is concerned. All God wants is our best, however much— or little—that might be.

These size-obsessed folks need to remember the story of the widow's mite. It probably wouldn't hurt, either, if they took up golf, where they'd learn the lesson that the short putt that saves the par is as important as the long drive that sets up the hole. It may not look as pretty or require as much athletic talent, but it means not one iota less.

Long or short, a stroke is a stroke. They all count the same, in faith as in golf.

17

Keeping Our
Amateur Status

". . . that Christ may dwell in
your hearts through faith, as
you are being rooted and
grounded in love . . . that
you may be filled with
all the fullness of God."
Ephesians 3:17, 19

Keeping Our
Amateur Status

THE SAND wedge tipped me off. Its grooves were worn almost completely away, the result (I was to learn) of its owner's spending many hours in the practice bunker. I was not surprised, then, by the huge drives, the radar irons, and the pinpoint putts I was privileged to watch him execute that day; anyone who practices sand shots is bound to be a serious golfer. Indeed, my friend who set up the game alerted me beforehand that Jim would be the best golfer I'd ever played with. He didn't exaggerate. I discovered besides that Jim was delightful company, not the least puffed up about his regal game and in no way patronizing toward us golfing mortals, who watched in awe.

Not long into the round I asked Jim the question he had surely fielded many times before: Did you ever

consider turning pro? He no doubt enjoyed my incredu-
lous expression when he told me he was presently in
the midst of the Professional Golf Association's lengthy
procedure for giving up his professional standing in order to regain his amateur status. It seems that after
four years as a scholarship golfer in a big-time college
program, Jim decided to try his hand as a touring pro.
Though he never got all the way to the big tour, he did
manage to make a living for several years on the satellite
circuit in Florida.

Like most duffers, I have fantasized about the professional golfer's life—consummate game, perpetual day in
the sun, maybe even fame and fortune—and wondered
why anyone who had a shot at such a life would give
it up. As Jim patiently explained, he hadn't lost confidence in his ability; neither did he use the term "burn-
out" to describe his decision. He just said the insight
came one day that his beloved game had evolved into a
job, a way to make a living, and had lost something in
the process. In his mind and heart he loved golf as much
as ever, only the daily grind of working to make a living
at it diminished his ability to taste its joy. At that point
he knew he had a decision to make: either continue to
play golf professionally and risk losing his love for it
altogether or return to golf as a game and find some
other way to make a living. He chose the latter, as he
said that day, without a subsequent regret.

In a culture that so lionizes "the professional," it is refreshing to hear a story like Jim's. It reminds us that the word *amateur* is not properly defined as one who is lesser than a professional. According to the Latin from which it comes, an amateur is one who pursues a particular activity for the sheer love of it. It has nothing to do with compensation or level of proficiency; it has everything to do with passion, joy, and commitment. An amateur does what he does because he loves it, pure and simple. The fact that he gets no pay, or that he never develops his prowess beyond a certain point, is immaterial.

Christians, take note. When it comes to living out our faith, we best conceive of ourselves as amateurs, people whose chief motivation for the practice of Christianity is love. We are to be "rooted and grounded in love," as the writer of Ephesians puts it, if we would "be filled with all the fullness of God." We don't follow the Christian path because we think we have some special knack for it, or because it seems a respectable thing to do, or because we covet some reward we suspect it might bring. Rather, we make this commitment because we love God with a love so strong we cannot do otherwise. A Christian is the quintessential amateur.

Ordained clergy especially need to hear this word. As one myself, I know how easy it is for a minister to regard his vocation as a profession. To the extent this helps clergy develop the various skills necessary for their work and build an ethic for their conduct, this is good; however, when such considerations threaten to supplant love for God with concern about competence or status or livelihood, overprofessionalization has occurred. It's time for that minister to take steps to regain his amateur status. That doesn't necessarily mean surrendering the credentials of ordination, but it does mean restoring the proper sense of priority: love of God first, then competence, ethic, livelihood, and so on.

There's a message here for laity, too, particularly those who take their faith so seriously as to become quasi-clergy themselves. These are the folks who give unstintingly of their time, talent, energy, and resources for the sake of the community of faith. Those who make such expenditures as an unself-conscious expression of their love for God are the purest examples of Christianity to be found. On the other hand, when such efforts are undertaken ostentatiously, when they are accompanied by the expectation of some tangible reward, when they run hot and cold depending on the kind of response they generate, something's wrong. Faith has become too much duty, not enough love. When a layperson feels this going on within, he needs to take stock. Somehow, the blessing of his amateur status has been lost, and it needs to be reclaimed.

It all turns on remembering the root meaning of that

word; an amateur is a lover, one who does something out of the highest possible motivation. Given that definition, there is no more honorable designation a person can carry in any field of endeavor. Jim learned that to be true in golf, which is why he had the courage to take the unusual step of regaining his amateur status.

May we Christians, lay and clergy alike, be so wise that we are proud to consider ourselves amateurs—lovers of God—above all.

18

Power

"For God's foolishness is wiser
than human wisdom, and
God's weakness is stronger
than human strength."
1 Corinthians 1:25

Power

GOLF CONFOUNDS conventional wisdom. Consider, for example, the matter of power. In most sports power is equated with great size and strength. Hulk Hogan in wrestling, Reggie White in football, Cecil Fielder in baseball, Charles Barkley in basketball—each epitomizes power, and there's not a runt in the litter.

What about golf? Are its long hitters ever suspected of popping steroids? Hardly. Every once in a while a large man like George Bayer may distinguish himself for his distance, but for the most part, the excellent golfers who happen to be long hitters seldom cast imposing physical shadows. Ben Hogan, the author of *Power Golf,* would be nicknamed "Hulk" only in jest. The great golfing triumvirate of the 60s—Palmer, Player, and Nicklaus—would be dwarfed by the front lines of most of today's high school basketball teams. One of the more successful golfers on the senior tour, Chi Chi Rodriguez, has made a career of outdistancing opponents who tower over him. The longest player on the present scene is John Daly, who would never be mistaken for a body-builder.

The moral is, you need not be a gorilla to have a powerful golf game. More than anything else, timing—getting everything in the right place at the right moment—is the key, and persons of small to average stature seem especially blessed with this attribute. So golf confers no special advantage on big people. Indeed, unless the big golfer has exquisite timing and unusual flexibility, his bulk could be more curse than blessing.

In this respect golf illustrates God's preferred mode of operation in the world, as the Bible shows repeatedly. While we affirm that God is omnipotent, we also acknowledge biblical testimony that God's great power most often comes camouflaged in human weakness. Examples abound. God's chosen nation issues from Abraham and Sarah, a barren couple beyond child-conceiving years. Moses, who has no distinctive background aside from being an orphan and a shepherd, becomes God's instrument of deliverance for the Hebrew people. The conquest of Jericho is accomplished by a ridiculously small, outmanned, and ill-equipped band of soldiers. One of the valiant leaders of the Hebrews during the period of the judges is Deborah, a woman. The destroyer of Goliath, the giant Philistine warrior who had cowered King Saul's army, is David, a shepherd boy armed only with slingshot and stones. The multitude of Baal prophets on Mt. Carmel, despite their numbers and political backing, is routed by a single servant of God, Elijah.

And if the point is not sufficiently made by these and many similar Old Testament stories, then surely it is driven home with the appearance of Jesus of Nazareth. He is the ultimate expression of God's power, yet he comes in startling humanity. Born in a stable, raised in a carpenter's home, baptized in the manner of any seeker requiring purification, subject to temptation, misunderstood by his followers, hated by the leaders of his religion, deserted by those who seemed to love him, treated as a political pawn, executed as a criminal—this is the Son of God. Because we know the tomb was empty on Easter Sunday, we sometimes forget that God's ultimate self-revelation to the world, Jesus Christ, came in human form—a servant, disdaining the privilege of divinity in order to put a human face on the truth about God's power.

This confounds, and it's meant to do so. Paul says boldly that God acts in ways that appear foolish in the world's eyes precisely for the purpose of shaming, in the hope of converting, the world. As far as God is concerned, power has nothing to do with size, wealth, status, prestige, intellect, military might, political clout—characteristics we admire. Rather, God's sense of power reposes in humility, obedience, justice, hope, faith, and above all, love. To this there are many witnesses, but none are more compelling than the crucified Savior, who will not let us forget that God's power most frequently comes in the form of weakness.

Obviously, this carries important implications for the way we practice our faith. If we truly believe that God lodges in, identifies with, and works through persons and institutions the world considers marginal, then we're going to commit ourselves to solidarity with them; we're going to cherish, protect, and serve them. Mostly, we will open ourselves to what they can show us of the power of God. If the world deems us foolish, that's okay; indeed, it's probably a sign that we're on the right track.

And if we are the meek of the earth ourselves, we rejoice, for the evidence is indisputable. The world may hold us in contempt, but we are precious in God's sight, precious to the point of being God's chosen instruments time and time again.

Americans may stumble over this, because in our culture we tend to identify power with raw size and strength. Our games give us away at this point, as they so often glorify these attributes. That's where we golfers might be able to help. In our game you don't have to be a gorilla to play powerfully—just like in Christianity.

About the Author

Dr. John Freeman is an ordained United Methodist minister in the South Carolina Annual Conference. He presently serves as Assistant Professor of Practical Theology at Emory University's Candler School of Theology. He holds degrees from Wofford College, Yale Divinity School, and the Lutheran Theological Southern Seminary.

Freeman, who lives in Atlanta, does most of his golfing in the Southeast, and he plays to an eight handicap.